german shepherd dog

understanding and caring for your pet

Written by
Gill Ward & John Ward

german shepherd dog

understanding and
caring for your pet

Written by
Gill Ward & John Ward

Pet Book Publishing Company

Bishton Farm, Bishton Lane, Chepstow, NP16 7LG, United Kingdom.

Printed by Printworks Global Ltd., London/Hong Kong

The 'he' pronoun is used throughout this book instead of the rather impersonal 'it', however no gender bias is intended.

ISBN: 978-1-906305-57-4
ISBN: 1-906305-57-9

Acknowledgements

The authors would like to thank our good friend Michele Brusey for her invaluable help in typing the manuscript, and contributing photographs. Thanks also to members from the Cornwall branch of the British Association for German Shepherd Dogs for allowing their dogs to be photographed for this book.

The publishers would like to thank the following for help with photography: Katrina Stevens (Kesyra), Gill and John Ward (Belezra), and Guide Dogs for the Blind Assocation.

Contents

Introducing the German Shepherd

The German Shepherd Dog is one of the most popular of all breeds. His natural presence and noble good looks, coupled with his versatility as a working dog and loyal family companion, is the reason why the breed is held in such high regard.

No other breed is as effective in so many widely varying situations, living and working alongside man. German Shepherds are employed worldwide as police dogs, using their tracking and searching skills, and their courage defending their handlers, as well as chasing and detaining criminals. The German Shepherd is also widely used by the armed services, being adaptable enough to cope with foreign postings.

The breed has distinguished itself as a search and rescue dog. The amazing scenting ability, sharp hearing, outstanding endurance, and the weather-resistant coat of the German Shepherd enables him to cope with extreme weather and environmental conditions, searching for avalanche, earthquake or explosion victims. He has saved many lives due to his determination in searching for human scent in atrocious conditions.

The versatility of a German Shepherd's character, such as being calm, biddable and confident, has seen him in the role as a guide dog for the blind and as an assistance dog. German Shepherds have served us faithfully throughout history – this is a multi-talented dog and a truly unique breed.

Companion dogs

The German Shepherd is prized as a working dog, but it is a fact that the majority of Shepherds are in pet homes where they live stimulating and fulfilling lives. However, before you take on a German Shepherd, you must first decide whether you can meet his specific needs.

The German Shepherd is capable of great loyalty and devotion. He is alert and responsive to training, which he will need whether it is formal obedience or just for good manners. He is a fun dog who can show pure joy just messing about with his owner. His lively enthusiasm requires guidance not inhibiting, so, as a prospective owner, you need to be calm, assertive, understanding and consistent in your interactions with him. He will get on well with children as long as he is well socialized with sensible youngsters. He will give you companionship, affection and a sense of security, as well as encouraging you to take plenty of exercise.

German Shepherds are slow to mature, especially mentally, so puppy mischievousness may be retained into adulthood. Your dog will need plenty of mental stimulation to keep his active mind from finding its own entertainment. This may include chewing the furniture, digging up the garden or barking – he can be very creative when trying to relieve his boredom.

German Shepherds are very motivated by movement, which is why the use of toys or balls is a useful training aid, but this characteristic can become a problem. Moving objects, such as other dogs, joggers or cars, may attract his attention and he could be tempted to give chase. This is why early training is very important.

This is a breed that can be very demanding on your time and budget. You will need to make sure that your garden is secure, which means fencing at least 5 ft (1.5 m) high, as a German Shepherd is very agile and can clear heights that other breeds of the same size may not consider jumping. You must also be aware of how much it will cost to keep a large dog such as a German Shepherd, and ensure you can take this responsibility on and afford to do it comfortably.

The Shepherd's double waterproof coat will moult, usually twice a year, but to some degree he can shed hairs almost continuously. You must therefore be prepared to groom your dog regularly and buy a good-quality vacuum cleaner to minimize the amount of dog hair around the house.

German Shepherds can become over-attached to one person, so it is vital to recognise the huge commitment involved in socializing a puppy with a variety of people. It is also important that all the family is happy to have a German Shepherd and share in the daily care.

Developing the breed

There are hundreds of different dog breeds and many have their roots in the very distant past. However, the German Shepherd is a relatively young breed, developed in Germany at the end of the 19th century.

Its story began as a herding dog, but with the vision of one man who developed the breed's mental and physical qualities, the German Shepherd found his place as a true partner to mankind.

In rural Germany, farmers used a variety of herding dogs, and although the dogs shared similar characteristics, such as intelligence, strength and endurance, they varied in appearance depending on the region. The sheepdogs working in the highlands and the hills were small, stocky grey dogs with erect ears; the sheepdogs working on the plains were larger and more athletic, able to trot effortlessly all day on the flat terrain.

In 1891 a small group of enthusiasts formed the Phylax Society with the aim of standardizing the herding breeds. In fact, this group was short-lived, but the idea of developing a type of dog, known today as the German Shepherd Dog, was initiated.

The first German Shepherd Dogs

Captain Max von Stephanitz, who is known as the 'father of the breed', was an enthusiastic supporter of the German Shepherd Dog. He was impressed by the breed's herding heritage, intelligence, workability and strength of character. He established the Society of the Verein für Schäferhunde (SV), in April 1899. This was the first breed club for the German Shepherd Dog, and the SV continues to run the largest breed club in the world.

The very first German Shepherd Dogs were primarily bred to perform the duties of guarding flocks. It was only as the breed developed, while, at the same time, the number of flocks decreased, that they were used for other duties. Their sheer physical strength and versatility, combined with their resistance to bad weather and climate changes, made them excellent working dogs as well as outstanding companions. Soon they were being used by the police, and were entering civilian police dog trials with the help of the SV. In 1902 the SV published the first rules for police and service dog training.

Left: *The breed is used by the police and the armed services throughout the world.*

The outbreak of the First World War saw the full potential of the breed, working in the role of service dogs. Daily tasks included dispatch carrying, which sometimes involved carrier pigeons attached to a body harness, and cable-laying assistance. Also, essential food supplies were carried between the trenches when under enemy fire. These were just some of the courageous feats these dogs performed.

The international shepherd

Soldiers returning to the USA and Britain after the First World War told tales of the wonderful dogs they had seen in action, and some even brought German Shepherd Dogs back with them. One such soldier was Lee Duncan, who imported a German Shepherd called Rinty to the USA. He saw the dog's remarkable potential and after specialised training, Rin Tin Tin became a movie star, and did much to popularize the breed.

Unfortunately the breed paid a price for its sudden upturn in popularity. Unscrupulous breeders started producing puppies on a mass scale, with little regard to their soundness, both with regard to temperament and conformation. It took many years for breeders, on both sides of the Atlantic, to restore the breed to its best.

Naming the breed

Following the First World War, there was considerable anti-German feeling, which reflected badly on the newly imported German Shepherd Dogs. In the USA, the name was changed to Shepherd Dog, and in the UK it was known as the Alsatian Wolfdog.

In 1931, the American Kennel Club considered that hostility toward Germany had abated sufficiently to restore the name to German Shepherd Dog. However, in the UK, the breed was known as the Alsatian for many decades, and it was not until 1974 that it became known by its true name.

The German Shepherd today

Now the breed is well established worldwide, and the modern German Shepherd has evolved into one of the most versatile of all breeds. His striking appearance draws admiration in the show ring and his working ability is prized in a variety of disciplines.

He remains breed of choice for the police and security services where his courage, loyalty, intelligence and tracking skills are put to the test; he is highly valued as an assistance dog, and he competes with distinction in many of the canine sports, such as obedience, tracking, and agility. It is this unique combination of good looks, versatility and outstanding companionship that makes the breed so very special.

The German Shepherd bonds closely with people and makes an outstanding Guide Dog for the Blind.

What should a Shepherd look like?

The Breed Standard is a written description of the ideal German Shepherd Dog, describing the physical aspects, temperament and character to ensure all the qualities adopted to produce this legendary breed are retained.

It is used as a blueprint by breeders and judges so that only the very best dogs are selected and used to produce future generations. Here we look at the main points of the Breed Standard:

General appearance

The German Shepherd Dog is a working dog that is alert and well balanced. Ideally, he is of medium

6103
BACCARA

size and strong, with a well-muscled, powerful build. He is slightly longer than his height. The male is larger, giving a clear impression of masculinity over the femininity of the female.

Temperament

A German Shepherd's temperament is lively but should be obedient and adaptable. He is highly intelligent and very active. The ideal German Shepherd is a calm, confident, and loyal dog, but he must also display courage and resilience in the defence of his owner and possessions. He should be observant and a good housedog, friendly with his family and children, and with other dogs, and always at ease with people in general. He should never be aggressive, nervous or shy.

Points of anatomy

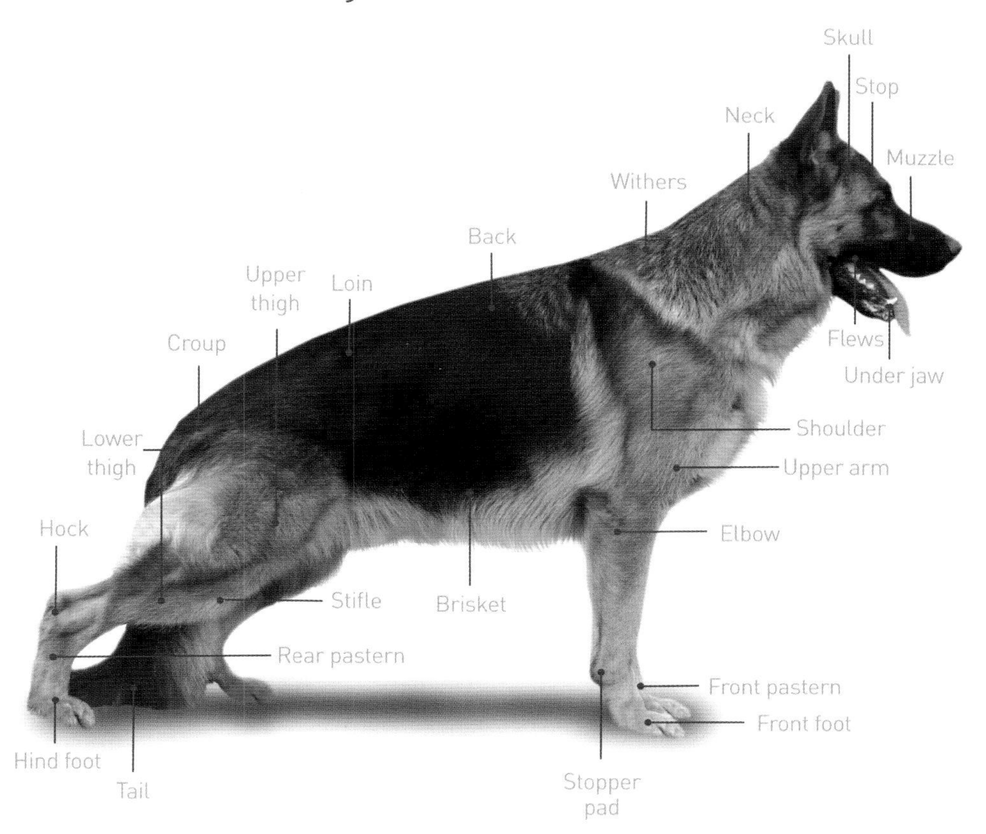

Head and skull

The German Shepherd's head should be proportionate to the body without being coarse, too fine or over long in the muzzle. The general appearance should be slightly broad between the ears. The forehead should be very slightly domed with little, or, at the most, only a slight trace of centre furrow when viewed from the front or side.

The top of the head should be equal to 50% of the whole length of the head when viewed from above, tapering from the ears to the tip of the nose, running into a wedge-shaped, strong muzzle. The width of the skull should be equal with the length, and, in the case of males, slightly stronger than females. The muzzle should be strong with tight lips.

The eyes are medium-sized and almond-shaped. They should not be round or protrude, and should be as dark as possible, giving a lively, intelligent and self-assured expression.

The ears should be medium-sized, firm in texture and broad at the base. They should be set high, carried erect, almost parallel – not pulled inwards or tipped – tapering to a point, open at the front, and should never give the impression of being soft or loose, which would cause them to hang forward or lean over sideways.

The jaws should be strongly developed with a perfect, regular and complete scissor bite, i.e. the upper teeth closely overlapping the lower teeth, and set square to the jaws. The teeth should be healthy and strong, consisting of 20 in the upper jaw and 22 in the lower jaw. Full dentition is desirable, allowing the German Shepherd to grip securely.

Neck

The neck is fairly long, strong, with well-developed muscles, free from throatiness. It should be carried at a 45-degree angle to horizontal, raised when excited, lowered at fast trot.

Right: *The typical expression of the German Shepherd is lively with an air of self assurance.*

Forequarters

The shoulder blades should be long and set sloping (45°), lying flat to the body. The upper arm is strong and well muscled, joining the shoulder blade at approximately 90°.

The forelegs are straight from the pasterns to the elbows when viewed from any angle. Pasterns should be firm, supple and slightly angulated. The length of the foreleg should slightly exceed the depth of the chest.

Body

The body length should exceed the height at the withers by a ratio of 10 to 9 or 8.5, which is measured from the point of the breast bone to the rear edge of the pelvis. The topline runs without any visible break from the set of the neck, over the well-defined withers, falling away slightly in a straight line to the gently sloping croup.

The chest is deep, and is approximately 45- 48% of the total wither height. The ribs should be long and well formed without being barrel-shaped or too flat. The back should be firm and strong and well muscled. The withers are long and high, sloping slightly from front to back. The croup is slightly sloping at approximately 23°.

The shoulders are long and sloping and lie close to the body. The forelegs are straight from the pasterns to the elbows.

Hindquarters

The hindquarters are the powerhouse of the dog. They should be strong, broad and well-muscled, enabling effortless forward propulsion. The upper and lower thighs are of approximately equal length and should meet at an angle of about 120°.

The forequarter angles should correspond with the hindquarters. The hocks should be short, firm, and strong to give firmness and endurance in movement.

Feet

The feet should have rounded toes, well closed and arched. Pads should be well cushioned and durable. The nails should be short, strong and dark in color.

Tail

The tail should be bushy-haired and reach at least to the top of the hocks, but not beyond the middle of the hock joint. When at rest, the tail should hang in a gentle sabre-like curve; when moving, the tail will become raised, ideally never above the level of the back. When very excited or playing, the tail might be raised higher.

The body length should exceed the height at the withers – the highest point of the shoulders.

Movement

As a trotting dog, the movement follows a sequence of steps in a diagonal pattern, moving foreleg and opposite hindleg forward simultaneously. Well-balanced limbs and good proportions allow for an effortless, far-reaching gait. The German Shepherd is capable of maintaining this pace for long periods of time, which was required for his original function as a herding dog.

Below: *When moving, the German Shepherd should show an effortless, far-reaching gait.*

Coat and color

The German Shepherd should have a thick undercoat with an outer coat consisting of straight, hard, close-lying hair as dense as possible. Long coats with undercoat can now be shown at some Breed Specialty shows. Any coat without an undercoat is a fault.

Colors can be all black, black saddle with tan, or gold to light grey markings, as well as all grey, with lighter or brown markings, known as sable. The undercoat is grey or fawn. Color in itself is of secondary importance, having no effect on a dog's character or fitness for work. Whites, albinos, blues and livers are not accepted within the Breed Standard, although puppies of these colors can be born occasionally and make perfect companion dogs. The nose must be black in all colors.

Size

The ideal height for the German Shepherd is: males 63 cm (25 ins) and females 58 cm (23 ins). A difference of 2.5 cm (1 ins) either above or below the ideal height is allowed.

Facing page:
Telling the difference: Black and gold (left), sable (right).

Summing up

It is important to bear in mind that the Breed Standard describes the 'perfect' German Shepherd Dog. Breeders should aspire to produce dogs that conform as closely as possible to this written blueprint as it describes the essential German Shepherd Dog.

This page: *White German Shepherds crop up occasionally in litters, but the color is not accepted in the Breed Standard.*

Facing page: *Black is one of the accepted colors for German Shepherds.*

What do you want from your Shepherd?

Over the many years that we have been involved with German Shepherds, we have met a large number of people who have also chosen to share their lives with the breed. Most have found this partnership a deeply rewarding experience, but sadly there have been a few owners that have made the wrong choice because a German Shepherd was not the breed compatible with their lifestyle or experience.

Most German Shepherds that end up in an unsuitable home have been chosen by people who simply liked the look of the breed and had not considered the inherent behavior typical to the German Shepherd. Prior research to gain some general knowledge about the German Shepherd will help you decide if it is the breed for you, and will guide you towards selecting the puppy best suited to your lifestyle.

The German Shepherd is one of the most versatile of all breeds, and although he is the dog that can do it all, it will be in your best interests to decide exactly what you want from your dog.

Companion dog

If you want a Shepherd purely as a pet, you still want a healthy, good-looking representative of the breed, but you will not need to worry about the finer points that are required in a show dog. In terms of temperament, you should be looking for a more laid back individual that does not have the strong drive of those bred specifically to work.

Working dog

Do you have ambitions to get involved in one of the canine sports, such as competitive obedience, tracking, agility or Schutzhund?

If this is the case, you should go to a breeder who has produced dogs specifically for the discipline you have in mind. In this way, you stand the best chance of owning a dog that has the motivation – and the ability – to compete at the highest level.

Taking on a Shepherd with working potential requires a lot of commitment from you, as this will be the type of dog that needs to be mentally stimulated. You will have to set time aside for his training – and not give up when the going gets tough or if you find something else to do. A German Shepherd has outstanding working potential, but he does need your time, your patience and your guidance to get the best out of him.

Right: *If you plan to work your German Shepherd, look for a bold, inquisitive puppy who wants to play.*

Show dog

To help you make the best choice of puppy, study the Breed Standard and learn as much as possible about training a dog for showing in conformation classes. The best chance of owning a dog of show quality is to go to a breeder who specializes in breeding show dogs and has achieved a reputation for producing top-class dogs that are sound in both mind and body.

A reputable breeder will do their best to help select the right puppy. However, they cannot guarantee the puppy will be a successful show dog, as even a very promising puppy can change as he grows. For example, you cannot tell if an eight-week-old puppy will have missing adult teeth or if there will be a fault in the ear carriage – both of which would end his show career. However, this would not be a problem for a pet dog.

The parents' show record, health credentials and breeding history should all be taken into account and, remember, a show puppy deserves the same love, attention and socializing as a pet puppy.

What your Shepherd wants from you

Every breed of dog has its own special needs, but the German Shepherd is one of the more demanding. This is a highly intelligent dog, built on athletic lines, with a high degree of energy. He has a strong work ethic and will not thrive unless you, his owner, are willing to spend time training him, socializing him and exercising him. This is equally applicable regardless of whether you own a show dog, a working dog or a companion.

Exercise

Most people are attracted to the German Shepherd for his intelligence, his good looks, and his temperament. Hopefully, you are also looking for a companion to keep you fit and active, because this is a breed that needs regular and varied exercise on a daily basis – regardless of the weather.

A quick walk along the streets on a lead with just a run at weekends is not enough. He will need a mixture of energetic free-running in a safe, suitable area, games such as retrieving a ball or finding hidden toys, and exploring new places with you, such as woodlands, beaches and the countryside.

The amount of exercise a German Shepherd requires will depend on his age and fitness. An adult will need at least an hour of interesting and energetic exercise a day. Do not think that leaving him out in the garden alone is adequate – apart from chasing the birds, he will probably just wander around at a snail's pace, sniffing as he goes. This will not provide sufficient exercise or mental stimulation; owner participation is definitely required.

On the other hand, it is vitally important that puppies are not over-exercised. Your pup may seem to have boundless energy, but you need to bear in mind that his joints are still developing and his bones have not calcified. A growing puppy that is given strenuous exercise can do irreparable damage to his body.

Socialization

This is an on-going process, but the most important work is done during the first 18 months' of your Shepherd's life. In order for a dog to live in a family, and in the larger community, he must develop the confidence to cope with everything he comes across. This means that he must take all situations in his stride, reacting calmly in different and unfamiliar environments, and meeting people, and other dogs, without nervousness, apprehension or aggression.

It is your job to educate your Shepherd by taking him out and about so that he can get used to all the sights and sounds of the modern world. This is vital work, as your Shepherd needs to learn the social skills which will make him a model canine companion.

For more information on what is involved, see page 108.

Training

Some owners assume that training a German Shepherd is only for people who want their dog to perform formal obedience in competitions. In fact, training is all part of building a close bond with your dog, as it is essentially a two-way communication process. It would be simple if dogs and people spoke the same language, but as dogs have their own life values and body language, it is important that you have an understanding of how dogs communicate and learn.

Using dog-friendly training methods in a consistent, clear and fair manner is the key to successful training. Your training method does not only affect the behavior you want your dog to perform, but it can affect the dog's ability to learn in the future.

Whatever training you undertake with your German Shepherd, look on it as teamwork, developing a relationship based on trust and respect on both sides.

Other considerations

Before you start searching for a German Shepherd, you should narrow your choice so you know exactly what you are looking for.

Male or female?

A question we are often asked is: will a male or a female make the better pet? The simple answer is that both males and females can be equally loyal family companions with the right socializing and training. We feel that there are several important considerations that could determine your final choice of male or female.

The male is significantly larger and stronger and will be more likely to challenge authority, especially during the adolescence phase, as he will experience an upsurge in the male hormone, testosterone. When adult, he can be quite competitive, even aggressive, with other males, but he usually gets on with females.

The male (pictured left) is a bigger, more powerful animal than the female (right).

The female is smaller and usually less territorial. She is often more affectionate and biddable, so perhaps easier to manage for the first-time owner or a family with young children. She will come into season (estrous) on average twice a year for a period of three weeks. She may show behavioral changes during this time, associated with the hormonal changes she is experiencing. This can range from being more affectionate to being a little sensitive or excitable.

To avoid an unwanted pregnancy, a female must be kept away from amorous males during her season. Of course, she could be neutered (surgical removal of the ovaries and uterus, known as spaying). This will eliminate the inconvenience of the seasons and has a number of associated health benefits.

More than one?

If you already have a dog and you are planning to get a puppy, the general advice is to choose the opposite sex to the one you already have, as competition between the same sex can lead to friction later on. If you have a regular visitor to your home who brings a dog, follow the same advice of choosing the opposite sex. This will help the dogs to establish a harmonious relationship, especially when your puppy matures.

Unless you can keep them apart when the female comes into season, it would be wise to have one of them neutered. Apart from the risk of an unwanted litter, the male may go off his food, howl, urine-mark his territory (even in the house), or cause damage to the home in trying to reach the female if he picks up the scent of her in season. This is all natural behavior for an entire male. If the male is neutered (surgical removal of the testes known as castration), his instinctive desire to reproduce is removed.

Two together?

You may be tempted to take on two puppies at the same time – particularly if you see a litter of puppies and cannot make up your mind which one to choose. However, this is really not a good idea. You may think that rearing two puppies will be twice the fun but, in reality, it means twice the work. They will rely on each other, especially if they are from the same litter, and will naturally bond more closely together. This will make general training, and particularly bonding with you, very difficult.

A single puppy will learn to communicate and interact with his human family, which will make training easier and establish a much closer bond. Even if you bring a puppy into your home with an existing older dog, you need to remember that because humans and dogs are different species, it is natural for the puppy to bond strongly with the other dog, as they communicate in the same way and enjoy playing the same games. This could be to the exclusion of you.

If you decide you want two dogs, it is advisable to wait until the first dog has gone through the adolescence phase, has been well socialized, is under control, and you have formed a good relationship with him.

Resist the temptation of getting two puppies from the same litter.

An older dog?

Rearing a puppy is time-consuming and hard work, so an older dog may be a better option for you. Sometimes you can get a an older puppy from a breeder, who has 'run him on' for a few extra months to see if he will make the grade for showing. This youngster may make a highly suitable pet, with only a minor cosmetic fault that would make him unsuitable for the show ring.

The other option is to take on a rescued dog who needs another chance of finding a loving, forever home.

The advantage of taking on an older dog is you can assess his character and decide whether he is likely to fit into your lifestyle. The possible drawback is that the dog may have already formed some bad habits. You will need to find out as much as you can about the dog's history and temperament, as well as his general social behavior. For example:

- Is he good with men and women, and children of all ages?
- Does he get on with other dogs?
- Will he co-exist with small animals that are kept as pets?
- How does he behave in the home and in the car?
- What socializing has he had?

It can be immensely rewarding to rehome a dog, but it should not be undertaken lightly. In most cases, it is preferable if you have experience of owning dogs – and German Shepherds in particular – before you take on this challenge.

German Shepherd rescue societies always have older dogs in need of new homes. However, if you decide on a rescued dog, make sure the organization is recommended by a breed club.

If you are taking on an older dog, he will need kindness and consideration as he settles into his new home.

Sourcing a puppy

If you have decided the German Shepherd is the breed for you, the next serious consideration must be finding a reputable breeder.

The best place to start is with your national Kennel Club. Both the American Kennel Club and the Kennel Club in the UK have excellent websites that provide details of breed clubs, lists of German Shepherd Dog breeders, and also breeders that have puppies available. There are various schemes that have been designed to encourage reputable breeding and rearing practices, and genuine breeders will also adhere to a strict code of ethics and carry out health checks on their breeding stock.

Care must be taken in answering advertisements placed in local newspapers, pet shops or those on the Internet, unless they are to be found on the website of a well-established breeder. If many

different breeds of puppies are offered for sale at an establishment, this could be what is known as 'puppy farming' where unscrupulous people breed dogs in terrible conditions without any care for temperament or health issues.

Buying from an irresponsible breeder can have disastrous consequences, which will have a huge impact on you for years, so finding the right breeder is crucial. Knowledge of the breed varies widely in people breeding German Shepherds, from those who have very little interest in the breed (other than hoping to make money), to extremely conscientious breeders who have the welfare of the breed at heart and have many years of specialist knowledge on all aspects of German Shepherds.

A reputable breeder will be genuinely concerned that the home you can offer one of their puppies will be suitable. Not only will they be happy to answer all your questions, but they will ask you quite a few before agreeing to show you the puppies, or put you on a waiting list if they do not have any available at the time. Be very wary if the breeder does not seem interested in finding anything out about you and just wants to take a deposit to secure a sale.

Health issues

German Shepherds are generally a healthy breed, and, if they are fed a well-balanced diet and exercised correctly, they should live a long, healthy and happy life. However, there are a few genetic conditions that can affect the breed. Responsible breeders recognise this and take part in the various health-screening tests available to ensure these problems are kept to a minimum. Screening tests may be voluntary, but you would be well advised to go to a breeder that has all their breeding stock assessed.

For information on inherited conditions, see page 176.

Puppy watching

You will want to see the mother with her puppies.

Puppy watching

When you have found a breeder you are happy with and they feel you are a suitable owner, the all-important visit can be arranged.

For the first three weeks, the puppies do little but eat and sleep, so there will not be much to see. The mother will be closely bonded to her new babies and it is unfair to let strangers invade her privacy during these early weeks. Puppies are very vulnerable to disease, so most breeders will ask you not to visit after you have just been to another kennel, as infection can be transferred very easily.

The best time to view the puppies is about six weeks old, as, by this time, they will be aware of their surroundings and their individual characters will be emerging.

When you first arrive, check the puppies' living conditions. They should be clean, hygienic and smell fresh, with space to play and exercise as well as a cosy bedding area. A healthy puppy will be lively. His body will feel firm and well covered, but the skin should feel loose. The coat and ears will be clean and the eyes bright. Check that there are no dewclaws on the hind legs; they are left on the front legs on German Shepherds.

Meeting the puppies' mother is very important, because her behavior has a big influence on her offspring. She should be happy and confident, although she may not enthuse over you, as she may be more interested in her puppies. If she growls, backs away or is aggressive, her puppies may have picked up the same traits, so it could be a risk taking on one of them.

A reputable breeder will be happy to let you meet their adult dogs, which should be in good condition and greet you with wagging tails. If you watch how the breeder treats the dogs and how the dogs respond, it will give you an overall idea of how the puppies have been handled.

Choosing from the litter can be difficult as all puppies are irresistible, but the breeder will help you find the puppy that is most likely to suit your lifestyle. A caring breeder spends so much time with the puppies, they will know the individual characteristics of each one.

Family companion

If you are choosing a pet temperament is of paramount importance. The puppies should appear friendly, outgoing and happy to be around you. If you have children, watch their interaction, as some seem to have a natural affinity with young children. A puppy that is wary or runs away and hides is not a good choice. A very domineering, pushy individual who objects to being handled is equally unsuitable as a family companion. Both these extremes need an experienced owner. An average puppy, which is neither over-demanding nor nervous, is most likely to make a well-balanced pet

Working potential

You will be looking for a puppy that is confident and likes to play. He should be happy to approach you and curious if a new stimulus is introduced. He should be a natural retriever who likes to carry different objects and explore different environments. The puppy should be sociable and friendly, and interacts positively with the breeder.

Avoid a puppy that is shy, will not follow you or play with you, or shows signs of being hyperactive. If possible, see the puppy on his own – as well as with his littermates – to check his response. Hopefully, he will remain friendly and playful.

Below: *The breeder will have a detailed knowledge of all the puppies in the litter and will help you make your choice.*

Show potential

Puppies will change as they develop, but an eight-week-old puppy with show potential must have good conformation – the proportions of height to length should give a well-balanced appearance. He should move straight and sound when viewed from the front and behind. His back should look firm. He should have a scissor bite, with the upper jaw slightly overlapping the lower jaw. An overshot jaw would be a fault and, unless you are knowledgeable on the correct 'bite', you may not recognise this problem.

The ears may have started to lift slightly at the base, which is a good indication that they will come up. A male should have two testicles descended into the scrotum. A dog with one testicle cannot be shown.

The head of a male puppy should show strength; a female puppy should have a feminine expression. A fine skull or overlong muzzle in a puppy may not develop in the correct proportion to the body. Although color is of secondary importance in a companion or working dog, for a show dog a rich black and gold, quality coat is desirable. A white puppy should not be chosen if you hope to exhibit at any reasonable level of dog show as this color is a fault in the Breed Standard.

There may be one puppy who seems to say: "pick me".

Getting ready

Bringing your puppy home is an exciting time for you, but it can be unsettling for the puppy to cope with such an overwhelming change of circumstances. There are certain preparations you should make before collecting your puppy to help him settle in as smoothly and safely as possible.

In the garden

The garden must be securely fenced to a minimum height of 5 ft (1.5 m) to keep an adult German Shepherd in. The gate should have a lock and a sign requesting people to shut the gate. Check that the gate does not have any gaps that the puppy might squeeze through or under. If the gate is left only slightly open, a puppy could wriggle through with disastrous results.

Facing page: *A German Shepherd puppy will investigate everything he comes across.*

A puppy investigates new objects with his mouth, so small stones could be swallowed, as most puppies seem to delight in picking them up. Many house and garden plants are poisonous to dogs – rhododendron, wisteria, azalea, hyacinth, tulip bulbs, daffodil bulbs, poinsettia, and foxgloves among them. A full list is available on the Internet.

Toxic chemicals, such as pesticides, car oil and anti-freeze, need to be kept out of reach. Garden ponds seem to fascinate puppies, so if you have one, use a cover or protective fencing to make sure your puppy cannot accidentally fall in. If you have a swimming pool, make sure your puppy does not have access to it.

In the home

Your house will need the same safety inspection. Keep all detergents, cleaning chemicals and medicines stored well out of the puppy's reach. Ornaments and breakable items may need to be relocated. House plants at floor level will attract the puppy's attention. To stop him doing a bit of pruning, keep them – and anything else that could be a danger to the puppy – out of the way. Stairs can be very hazardous for a puppy. The use of a child gate at the bottom of the stairs or between rooms will restrict his access.

Cover or move electrical wires and keep children's toys out of reach. The puppy cannot discriminate between his chew toys and everything else. You can provide a box full of safe toys for him to play with, but if there is an electric cable to pull or a child's small toy tucked behind the sofa, you can be sure your puppy will find it.

Buying equipment

Before bringing your puppy home, have an enjoyable shopping trip to buy some of the essential items ready for the new arrival.

Dog bed

Wicker baskets, bean bags, duvets and wooden beds look attractive, but they are very chewable. The most practical type is the durable, rigid plastic bed, which is easy to wipe clean.

You should make sure that you a buy a bed that is big enough for an adult German Shepherd. Line it with bedding, such as a fleece blanket or fleecy veterinary-type bedding.

Crate

A crate is a very useful item of equipment, which can be used both as sleeping quarters and also as a safe den at times when you cannot supervise your puppy.

Line the crate with fleece bedding and add a few safe toys, and when your puppy is feeling tired, put him in the crate with some treats. Do not shut the door; let him go in and out as he wishes.

When the puppy is comfortable going into the crate, close the door for a short period. To start with, make sure your puppy can see you when he is in the crate. Gradually, he will use it as somewhere he can relax and sleep safely, as dogs are den animals.

Please note that a crate should not be used as a form of punishment, and neither a puppy nor an adult dog should be confined for long periods, except for overnight.

Food

The breeder will tell you which food your puppy has been reared on, so make sure you buy the same. Any change of diet must be done gradually to avoid the puppy having an upset stomach.

Bowls

A food bowl and water bowl made of stainless steel are tough and easy to clean. Avoid plastic bowls, as these will be chewed. German Shepherds seem to like playing with their bowls, so a non-spill water bowl would be a good idea.

Collar and lead

Puppies grow rapidly, so an adjustable, lightweight collar made of soft nylon is a good choice. As he grows, the best option is a half-check collar. This is made of nylon or leather and has a chain insert which can be adjusted to remain loose around the puppy's neck but will tighten just enough so that the puppy cannot slip out of it. You are required by law to have an owner identity disc attached to your dog's collar, even if he is microchipped.

A light, nylon lead will be fine for the first few weeks, but, as the puppy grows, it becomes increasingly uncomfortable to hold. A good-quality leather lead is the best option.

Toys

All dogs, especially puppies, love toys. Providing your puppy with his own toys to play with and to chew is essential. There is a good selection available and choosing is fun, but remember that a German Shepherd – even a very young puppy – has strong jaws. Check the toy to see that it is well made and does not have any small parts or pieces of fabric that could be chewed off and swallowed, possibly causing an intestinal blockage. Safe, durable toys include large knotted rope tuggers and natural rubber toys that are made for puppies to aid teething.

Grooming gear

The German Shepherd is a moulting breed, so keeping his coat in good order will require regular grooming. You will need an undercoat rake-type comb, a metal comb, a slicker brush and a bristle brush.

Finding a vet

An important person in your dog's life will be your vet. It is a good idea to do some homework before you bring your puppy home, so you can check out the facilities of veterinary practices in your area.

A vet who is knowledgeable about German Shepherds can be a real bonus, as he will be aware of conditions related to the breed. As you may be a client of the practice for many years, friendly and helpful veterinary staff, and a vet who takes the time to explain things and answer questions, is essential.

A puppy can be very destructive, so buy tough, durable toys.

Settling in

When you first arrive home, with your puppy, be careful not to overwhelm him. You and your family are hugely excited, but the puppy will be in a completely strange environment with new sounds, smells and sights.

Some puppies are very confident, wanting to play straight away and quickly making friends; others need a little longer. When you take your puppy indoors, let him investigate again. Show him where his bed is, which should be in a quiet, draught-free place, and show him his bowl. Fresh water should always be available.

Meeting the family

Help the puppy to establish good relationships with all family members by careful introductions. If you have children, do not let them chase the puppy when trying to make friends. Get them to sit quietly and let the puppy come to them. If they gently stroke him and give him a tasty treat, it will create

a positive association straight away. Remind the children not to pick the puppy up or encourage the puppy to play-bite them.

Children and puppies can be great friends if they are taught to respect each other. Supervise all interactions between them, because it is your responsibility to help develop a safe and happy relationship.

Give your puppy few days to settle in before you invite friends and relatives to see him, as all the attention can be too much for him and he will tire very quickly.

Introducing house pets

Introduce your puppy to the other house pets one at a time. Care must be taken, as the initial meeting can leave a lasting impression. If you have another dog, make sure you do not change the usual exercise, attention and feeding routine, as this may cause resentment.

Most adult dogs are very tolerant with puppies, but however trustworthy you think your dog is, the first introduction to the puppy must be controlled and well supervised. Dogs can be possessive over their toys, food, and their bed, so remove anything that could be a source of conflict.

Although it is important to protect the puppy, try not to interfere too much, as sorting out the hierarchy is essential to dogs (who are pack animals). Do not leave them alone together until you are absolutely sure they are getting on.

Once your older dog has accepted the puppy, they should settle down and work out their relationship. Just make sure that they both have time alone to rest and sleep undisturbed by each other.

A German Shepherd will generally get on with the family cat. Introductions should be made with the puppy restrained – either by being held or being put in his crate.

The cat must be able to move away from the puppy – preferably on to a higher surface – so that it does not feel trapped. Be careful, as a cornered cat may scratch the puppy and damage his eyes. By restraining the puppy when he first meets the cat, you can ensure that he doesn't discover how to make the cat run and the thrill of chasing it.

Encourage the puppy to look at you for a treat or play with a toy instead of paying attention to the cat.

Feeding

Your puppy will be accustomed to eating with his littermates, so eating on his own could affect his appetite. He may eat less than the recommended amount or eat the lot as fast as possible, as he is used to competing with his littermates at mealtimes.

Do not show any signs of anxiety by trying to coax him to eat, or overfeed him by giving him extra food because he cleared his bowl so fast. He will soon get used to eating alone as he settles into his new routine.

A puppy will quickly find his appetite when he has had a chance to settle.

The first night

The first few nights in a new home can be very distressing for a puppy. He has never been alone before and the routine he has lived by and accepted has gone.

There are different views about where the puppy should sleep. Some would advise that the puppy should be left in his bed or crate in the designated area, ignoring all crying and howling, to prevent bad night-time habits developing.

However, we feel this causes too much stress and anxiety to the puppy. The puppy will settle at night much quicker if he gets used to separation from the family (his pack) gradually.

If you have a crate for your puppy, put it in your bedroom and let the puppy sleep in it for the first few nights. A quiet word and your presence will reassure the puppy. Line the crate with plenty of paper and some cosy bedding at one end.

After a few days you will find that the puppy will adapt to his new surroundings. Then he should be confident enough to sleep on his own at night.

Your puppy may be slightly unsettled for a few days as he adjusts to his new night-time routine, but he should cope without it causing him too much concern, and eventually you will both have the benefit of an undisturbed night.

Give your puppy time and space to explore his new surroundings.

A rescued dog

It can be very rewarding to give a dog another chance for a happy life, but if you provide a home for a rescued adult or adolescent German Shepherd, he will need patience, kindness and common sense to help him settle in his new home. It is important to remember that everything will be strange and unfamiliar to your new dog, as he will have been used to different rules, different routines and different people.

Follow the advice given for a new puppy, allowing your rescued dog a chance to get to know his surroundings and the members of his new family pack. It may take him a few days or a few weeks to settle with his new family, during which time he may be slightly subdued. Many owners of rescued dogs say it takes a few months before a dog feels confident enough to show his true personality. Regardless of this, house rules and care plans need to be in place straightaway. A dog will find it much easier to settle if you are consistent in your handling right from the start. If your dog understands what is expected of him, he will get to grips with the new regime and will soon become an integral member of the family.

It can be very rewarding to rehome a German Shepherd and give him a second chance.

House training

New owners often express concern about house training their German Shepherd puppy, but this need not be a problem, providing you take the time to follow some practical guidelines.

Puppies have an instinctive tendency to move away from their sleeping area to go to toilet; this begins as early as three weeks old. Successful house training just develops this instinct. Puppies do not have much control of their bodily functions, and when they feel the need to relieve themselves, they really cannot hold on. You will need to be vigilant, consistent and very patient, especially in the first few weeks. Your new puppy will not know what is expected of him, so you must show him what you want. Give him frequent opportunities for toileting in a designated area of the garden, and try to avoid mistakes in the house.

You must establish a routine of taking your puppy to the same place in your garden at the predictable times that he will want to go to the toilet. Luckily, this is quite simple.

You must stay outside with him, and do not become impatient if he does not go straight away. Puppies are easily distracted – a leaf or blade of grass blowing in the wind will attract his attention. Give him time to settle down, say your chosen cue word, and praise him as soon as he performs. When you are unable to keep an eye on him, put him in his crate or playpen to restrict him temporarily and avoid house training setbacks.

When accidents happen

Accidents do happen and if you see your puppy about to squat, quickly interrupt him – clap your hands or call his name to get his attention. Then encourage him to follow you outside and reward him for finishing off in the garden. Never be cross with him, hit him, shout at him, or use any other harsh methods if he has an accident in the house. This will only confuse and upset the puppy, causing him to lose confidence in you and hide away instead of letting you know when he wants to go to the toilet.

Your puppy will need to go:

- Immediately after he wakes up.
- Soon after eating or drinking.
- First thing in the morning (no time for you to have a cup of tea first!).
- After any excitement, such as visitors arriving or the children coming home from school.
- After he has been playing or any stimulating activity.
- If you see him looking agitated, sniffing the ground, circling around.
- More or less every hour.
- As soon as he is let out of his crate or playpen.
- Last thing at night.

Choosing a diet

One of the important aspects of daily care is providing your dog with the correct nutrition. It is vital for his health and wellbeing to feed a good-quality, balanced diet.

A good-quality diet must contain essential nutrients, protein, fat, carbohydrates, vitamins and minerals in sufficient quantities to suit the different stages in his life – from puppyhood to old age. Fresh drinking water must always be available.

Commercial diets

Canned meat, semi-moist, pouch, biscuit mixers and complete, dry food are all convenient to use, but vary in quality depending on the ingredients. Super-premium, complete, dry food producers have researched extensively to provide nutritionally balanced diets, especially during the growth phase. It

Facing page: *Choose a diet to suit your Shepherd's age and lifestyle.*

is not necessary to add supplements; in fact, they may even be harmful. A food that contains the highest-quality ingredients is, of course, more expensive.

Natural diets

Diets that are home-made, such as BARF (Biologically Appropriate Raw Food), are based on feeding raw meaty bones (raw chicken wings) and raw food to emulate the lifestyle of the dog in the wild. Home-cooked meals will require you to source the fresh ingredients and prepare them. You may need to add vitamins, minerals or calcium to provide all the necessary nutrients your dog will need. You will need to acquire considerable knowledge of canine nutrition to ensure the correct amounts are added.

Feeding regime

Puppies have little stomachs and their digestive system is very sensitive, so you need to feed a high-quality, digestible food that is specially formulated for puppies. Your puppy will need four meals a day until he is around 12 weeks old; at this stage he can be fed three meals a day. From about six months, feed him twice a day.

If you are feeding a commercial food, follow the product's instructions and divide the daily ration by the number of meals you are feeding per day. It is important to remember that the feeding amounts given are a guide, and your puppy may need more or less depending on his activity.

Establish a routine that is convenient to you and try to feed your dog at the same time and place every day. He should be allowed to eat in peace and not be disturbed by people coming and going, or children playing with noisy toys near his bowl. If you have another dog, do not leave them unattended when they are being fed.

Bones and chews

To help relieve the discomfort of teething, we give our puppies large marrowbones to gnaw. It helps the removal of loose puppy teeth, and, at the same time, all the chewing works the jaw muscles, which appears to help the ears come up.

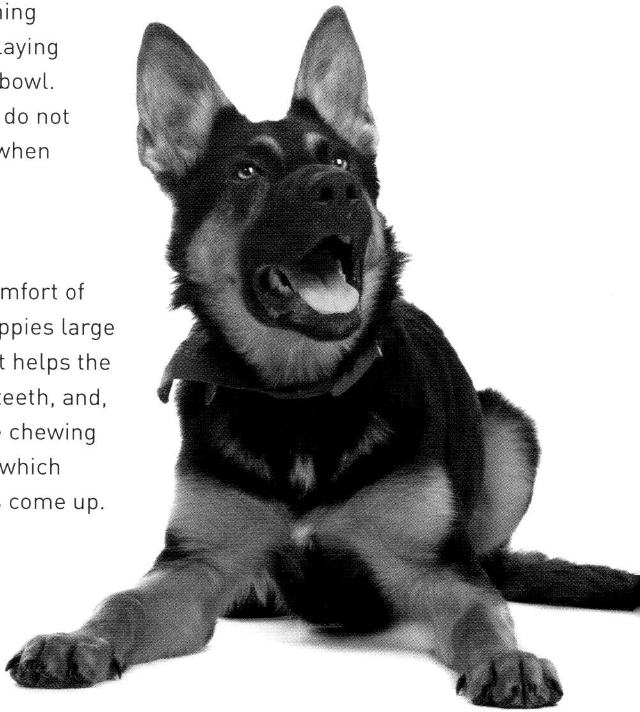

Right: *Monitor the amount you feed while your puppy is growing.*

We do not give bones to our adult German Shepherds, even though we know they would enjoy them. With their powerful jaws they would eat the bones rather than just chew on them, which could cause severe constipation. Some bones, such as turkey, pork or cooked chicken, should never be given to dogs as they splinter easily, causing intestinal blockage or cuts to the throat.

Rawhide chews are very popular, but a German Shepherd will quickly reduce them to a soft mush and try to swallow large pieces. Dogs have been known to choke to death on these. If you give bones or chews to your dog, always supervise him.

Ideal weight

Calculating the amount of food your German Shepherd will need on a daily basis to keep him fit and healthy will depend on his age, activity level and the environment he lives in. It is important to watch his weight; as a general guide, you should be able to feel his ribs but not see them.

Failure to provide enough food, or feeding a diet with a poor nutritional level to match the energy needs, will result in an underweight dog whose ribs are very visible and whose coat is dull and scurfy.

Photo © Metropolitan Police Dog Training Establishment.

Dangers of obesity

The idea that the overfed, fat, roly-poly puppy will make a bigger adult is mistaken. The accelerated growth and strain on the body could lead to serious malformations of the joints and bones.

Unfortunately, obesity in adult dogs is becoming widespread and with it comes an increase in weight-related medical problems.

A high body-fat percentage increases anesthetic and surgical risks. With increased body weight, there is more physical stress placed on the muscles, bones and joints, and this can result in severe arthritis and joint problems in later life.

Increased amounts of fat are also deposited around the internal organs, as in humans, and result in reduced function or dysfunction. Obesity can be a contributory cause of other conditions, such as diabetes, heart disease and breathing problems.

Bear in mind that you are responsible for your Shepherd's health and wellbeing, and by over-feeding you are literally killing your dog with misplaced kindness.

A dog that is the correct weight will live a longer, healthier life.

Caring for your German Shepherd

The German Shepherd is a relatively easy breed to care for, but it is important that you keep a close check on your dog, noting any changes – no matter how minor they are appear to be. If trouble is spotted at an early stage, the chances of a successful outcome are greatly increased.

Grooming

The German Shepherd has a double coat, comprising a dense undercoat and harsh-textured outer coat. He will need regular grooming to remove dead hair and to ensure the coat stays in good condition. During moulting, he sheds a large

amount of hair, so daily grooming, using your undercoat rake, will keep him looking tidy and will stop tufts of his fur coming out all over the carpet or anything else he brushes up against.

Long-coated German Shepherds are higher maintenance and will require almost daily brushing and combing to stop the coat from tangling and forming mats. To prevent a dull or dusty appearance to the coat, wipe your dog over with a velvet cloth or grooming glove.

It is a good idea to get your German Shepherd puppy used to being groomed. Choose a time when he is not too lively and playful. Brush him daily for just a short time, using a soft brush. Use gentle strokes from the head to the tail, and reward him for co-operating. He will soon get used to the procedure.

Bathing

Frequent bathing is not recommended, as this will strip the coat of its natural oils. If the coat is really dirty, or after a moult, a bath using a gentle dog shampoo may be needed. Make sure the water is not too hot or too cold, and avoid getting shampoo or water in your dog's eyes and ears. In general, a healthy puppy should not need bathing.

Teeth

You will need to be very gentle when you examine your puppy's mouth because, during teething, his gums will be sore. They may also be red and swollen. If a milk canine tooth remains in place as the permanent canine comes through, it can force the canine tooth to erupt further forward than normal; it will also leave the puppy with two sets of teeth. Consult your vet, as the baby canines may need removing.

Dogs build up tartar on their teeth, which can result in tooth decay and gum disease. Get your dog used to having his teeth cleaned from an early age, using a special dog toothpaste and soft brush.

Ears

Check the ears are clean; ear cleaners are available from the vet for routine use. Do not use cotton buds as you risk probing too deeply into the ear canal. Watch out for signs of redness, brown discharge or a bad smell, which may be the start of a problem. See Ear Infections, page 169.

There is an increased workload if you own a long-coated German Shepherd.

Nails

It is a good idea to accustom your puppy to having his paws touched by gently holding each paw, looking at his nails, and rewarding him with a small treat. This will help when you need to trim his nails.

If the nails have grown too long, you will need to trim the tip of each nail, using guillotine-type nail clippers. Trimming little and often is best, to avoid cutting the quick, which is the soft inner part which contains blood vessels. This is difficult to see in a German Shepherd's dark nails but, if accidentally cut, it will bleed and will be painful for the dog. If you are unsure about trimming your dog's nails, ask your vet or breeder to help.

The older German Shepherd

Many German Shepherds are quite active well into their veteran years; even so, it is wise to make some changes to your dog's care. Adjusting his diet to a specially formulated food for seniors will help prevent some of the age-related problems, such as obesity and constipation, and will be much easier for him to digest. A raised feeding bowl can make it easier for him, especially if arthritis is becoming a problem. You should also ensure he has comfortable, soft bedding to rest on.

The older German Shepherd will find it easier to cope with two or three shorter walks rather than one long walk. Keep a check on his water intake, and note any signs of coughing, limping or changes in behavior. Talk to your vet, who may suggest treatment to keep him more mobile and comfortable.

There are many treatments your vet can offer for age-related diseases, but there may come a time when an incurable illness or physical deterioration means your dog's quality of life has reached an unacceptable level. Making the decision to let him go is almost unbearable after sharing your life for so long with your faithful friend, but you must do what is best for your dog. Stay with him, stroking and talking to him as he slips away peacefully, and take comfort knowing you have taken care of your beloved pet's welfare to the very end.

Socialization

Every time you take your German Shepherd out, you are representing all of the breed. It is not difficult to raise your dog to be confident and sociable, but there are two contributing factors that will affect the outcome: the puppy's inherited traits and his life experiences.

You cannot alter his genetic make-up, but you can have a tremendous influence on his life experiences. Hopefully, the breeder has produced the correct character by selecting breeding stock for their temperament as well as health and looks, because this is the first important foundation for your puppy.

The home environment

Many of our household items can appear frightening to a small puppy. It is very important to accustom your puppy gradually to the sights and sounds of the television, the vacuum cleaner and the washing machine in a calm, controlled way. Care must be taken not to startle the puppy as he is habituated to your domestic environment.

Similarly, when you take your puppy out for the first few times, keep away from busy roads with cars and lorries speeding past; even bicycles can be a very frightening experience for a vulnerable puppy. A bad experience can set up a lifetime fear or phobia.

I find taking a puppy to a car park where vehicles are moving slowly, and playing with him at a distance from them, allows him to see and hear what is going on around him without feeling apprehensive or overwhelmed. It is also a great place for the puppy to see and meet people. Some will be in a hurry, and some may come and say hello to your puppy, so make sure you have some tasty treats to feed him as he meets someone new, so the experience is a rewarding one.

Socializing with other dogs

Dogs come in all shapes and sizes, and for your puppy to be sociable around other dogs he will benefit from meeting a variety of adult dogs with good social skills, used to interacting with unfamiliar puppies. Puppies need to learn

how to communicate with other dogs, as often their social skills are clumsy and extreme during dog-to-dog greetings. Great care must be taken that unfamiliar dogs do not frighten your puppy when you are in a public place. You must protect him from encounters with other dogs unless you are absolutely sure they will do him no harm.

Early encounters

The earlier a puppy has enjoyable encounters with things he will come into contact with later in life, the more sociable and well-balanced an adult he will grow into and be less prone to developing problem behaviors. As time goes on, new experiences will be viewed as normal – not strange or scary – providing the puppy has been given positive exposure to as much as possible before 12 weeks old.

Do not make the mistake of thinking that because your eight-week-old German Shepherd puppy is friendly and playful, you will not need to start socializing him yet. If you miss the early, important weeks, he will have a poor ability to develop his social skills. Socializing is an exciting time as you help your puppy to discover something new every day with your support and encouragement.

Let him familiarise himself with new experiences at his own pace, allow him to approach, investigate and even retreat if he is not quite sure of something. Do not overwhelm him; his natural curiosity will bring him forward to investigate, and then he can be rewarded.

Do not try to verbally reassure or soothe any fearful behavior. The puppy will interpret this as a reward for his behavior, and you will be, unintentionally, training him to become fearful. Instead, do not show any concern; jolly him along and use play to distract him and reduce his apprehension. If he seems fearful in many different situations, which he is unable to recover from quickly, ask your vet to recommend a behavioral trainer to help you.

Why train your German Shepherd?

Dogs are pack animals and see themselves as part of the family social structure. They live by instincts and by learning, during interactions with others, where their position is within the pack.

Status is very important to dogs. Most are born to be followers, but other more dominant characters instinctively would take on the role of leader. To live in harmony with your dog, you must be the pack leader and the dog's role is below all human members of the pack.

Establishing yourself as the pack leader does not mean you become a tyrannical dictator forcing your will on your dog. By thoughtful structuring of

everyday interactions and training, you demonstrate your leadership and gain your dog's respect and co-operation in a way that encourages him to naturally see you as pack leader. You give guidance, support, make the rules and provide a feeling of well-being. Training connects you with your dog as you discover the sheer joy of communicating and tuning into your dog's needs.

People wrongly say they do not need to train their dog because he is only a "pet". Training is about teaching your dog to be reliable when you take him out; he will travel well and be a well-behaved companion as he accompanies you to school, to the shops and on family outings. A German Shepherd enjoys learning new activities, and, with positive training methods, you will stimulate his active mind.

How dogs learn

The vast majority of your dog's behavior is the result of reinforcement. This term covers basically anything your dog likes: food, playing, toys, tone of voice, petting, access to the outside, access to a certain person – and one, most people do not consider, escaping from something unpleasant.

When training your German Shepherd, the reinforcement procedure should be as follows: your dog does something you like, and so you immediately do something your dog likes. This is a very powerful and fast method of training because if an action brings reward and pleasure, the dog will almost certainly do it again. If an action brings something unpleasant or nothing at all, then the dog is less likely to do it again.

For the dog to associate his actions with the consequences, timing is crucial. The consequences must be immediate as, unlike people, dogs do not have the ability to reason that something that happened earlier can result in something good or bad happening to them later.

Right: *The intelligent Shepherd enjoys the stimulation of learning new activities.*

Clicker training

Using positive motivation and reward training methods will produce a happy, co-operative dog.

The clicker is a useful training aid which serves to underline the behavior you want. It comes in different shapes, but it is a small, plastic device with a piece of metal inside that makes a sharp click when it is pressed. The sound of the click must be paired with food, or something the dog really likes, so he is able to associate the click sound with a reward, known as click and treat.

Once the clicker has been introduced properly, it is a very effective tool to mark the precise moment that the dog is performing the correct behavior. The click clearly indicates to the dog which behavior resulted in a reward.

Training guidelines

A German Shepherd is highly intelligent and capable of learning quickly. Regardless of whether he is a puppy or an adult, training will always be more successful if you take the time to do a little background research into developing and improving your handling skills. There are a few important guidelines that will enhance your ability to train your German Shepherd.

Evaluate the dog

Before every training session, check he is healthy, has been exercised (to relieve himself), and has not just been fed a big meal. Be aware of his temperament, drives, training experience, or if there are any environmental or behavioral issues.

Keep a close check on your dog when you are training to make sure he is showing a happy, positive attitude.

Be prepared

Evaluate yourself honestly, including assessing your physical and emotional state at each training session. Be flexible and ready to adapt training techniques to suit your dog or situation at any time. Know your own limitations. Respect the dog as a living, feeling individual. Understand the dog's body language and signals.

Be aware of the environment

Make sure the environment is likely to promote successful training. When teaching new commands, begin your dog's training without distractions, as this element may compete for the dog's attentive focus. Factors that can affect the dog should be taken into consideration, such as people and animal distractions, weather conditions, surrounding noise, and ground surface. Learn to anticipate distractions.

Get ready

Make sure the appropriate equipment for your training is readily accessible, including toys or food for reward, and a correctly fitted collar and lead. Use all equipment correctly and humanely.

Have a training plan

Draw up a clear plan for each training session, and be consistent with verbal commands and any body signals you intend using. Decide how you are going to pronounce the sound and tone of each command and consistently say each command in its own unique way every time it is used.

Use incremental training

Help the dog to understand what is required by breaking down the behavior into small, clear, progressive steps, making sure the dog is successful and confident at each step before moving on to the next. Continually evaluate the dog's reaction and be aware of its meaning.

Be adaptable and, if the dog is showing confusion or continually making errors, be prepared to back up the training to a level at which the dog was successful and break the required behavior into concepts the dog can understand. Be clear with commands, body motions and hand signals. Let the dog relax, while you think about the problem and come up with a solution.

Train in easy stages so your Shepherd understands what is required.

Establish reliability

Gradually build the dog's understanding of each command. The dog should respond correctly without hesitation before you add distractions, or increase distance or duration of the training. Only change or add one element at a time. Dogs are context-specific learners and do not generalize easily. This means they may have problems responding to training in a different environment, for example.

Correct training strategy ensures reliability – everywhere, every time, no matter what is happening. Sometimes return to an easier level to build confidence, but always reward the dog for responding correctly. He learns incrementally advancing skills during each training session, and responds reliably as increasingly challenging distractions are added.

Find motivation

Find out what your dog finds rewarding and use it. It might be food, a toy, a ball, verbal praise, or tactile praise. As most dogs like a variety of rewards, be creative and use different ones to keep the dog interested and trying to win his favorite reward. Verbal action rewards (which are words such as

Find a reward that your Shepherd really wants to work for.

"OK" or "That's it") release the dog to indulge in a behavior he wants and can be an excellent reward. Between or during formal exercises this gives the dog an enthusiastic release to interact and engage in play with the handler.

Know when to stop

A training session should end on a notable success that the dog has been well rewarded for. However, you should remain flexible to change your overall training plan if the environment or circumstances alter in a way that could adversely affect you or the dog. It is better to end or interrupt a training session as soon as you feel it is detrimental to successful learning for the dog, so that you can finish on a positive note.

By gradual and thorough training, patience and a calm attitude, doing your best to ensure all components are in place, you will set your dog up for success.

Make training sessions fun for you and your Shepherd.

First lessons

It is never too soon to start training – in fact, you can start almost as soon as your puppy has settled in his new home.

Wearing a collar

It is a good idea to get your puppy used to wearing a collar early on. Most puppies find it strange at first, so introduce it gradually. It should be neither too tight, to irritate or hurt, nor too loose, so that it could slip off.

- Put the collar on when the puppy is interested in something else – for example, during a play session. He may scratch at it to start with, but if you distract him with a toy or food, he will soon forget about it.
- Leave the collar on for 5-10 minutes for the first few times.
- When the puppy is not supervised, remove the collar in case it gets caught on something.

Lead training

Begin with a very gentle introduction to the lead when your puppy is happy wearing his collar.

- As soon as the lead is attached to the collar, encourage the puppy to you for a fuss and food treat.
- Take a small step and coax the puppy to move forward beside you. If he is reluctant to move, do not tug the lead or drag him, just encourage him again, offering a food treat to lure him forward. As soon as he moves forward, give him lots of praise. This will be enough for the first lead lesson.
- Repeat over the next few days, practising in the house and the garden. Gradually increase the number of steps that your puppy is taking with his lead attached. Always keep the lead loose, so that he does not get used to pulling you.
- If the puppy starts to pull, stand still, make an encouraging sound to get his attention and prompt him to come back to you, then praise and reward him.

Below: *The aim is for your Shepherd to walk on a loose lead – neither pulling ahead, nor lagging behind.*

- Take a step forward when the lead is loose. Get the puppy's attention on you by using his favorite toy or food held on your left side, just in front and above his nose. Get him to follow for a few paces. Say "Heel" as you reward him.

The correct position at your left side, the word "Heel" and the food reward must all happen at the same time for the puppy to understand where you want him to be, and to associate the reward with the behavior. These early lessons will imprint the idea of walking on a loose lead.

Mixed messages

Processing the meaning of words is not a natural behavior for a dog. The word has to be consistently associated with the action it is intended to cue, and then rewarded, for the dog to learn the meaning. Each word must have one meaning: for example, "Down" means lie down. It should not be used if you want the dog to stop jumping up.

Dogs are very sensitive to the tone and pitch of your voice, so when you have decided which words all the family will be using for commands and cues, the tone of voice must be consistent. It will be easier for the dog to associate the word with his actions if he hears it while he is displaying the behavior.

Come when called

Responding to the recall is one of the most valuable exercises you can teach your puppy. If he learns to come back on cue, he will enjoy a better quality of life as you will be able to give him free running exercise when it is safe to do so.

A good recall starts with your relationship with your dog; he must enjoy coming back to you because he finds you the most important and exciting thing in his life. Many owners say their dog always comes back when called, except if there are other dogs, people or rabbits around. What this actually means is: the dog only comes back when he is not interested in something else.

A reliable recall has to be taught. Do not assume that because your eight-week-old puppy happily rushes up to you when you call him that he knows what "Come" means. Very young puppies are naturally inclined to

stay close and come when called. Unless you reward the puppy for coming with praise, a treat or even a game with a toy every time he comes, the command "Come" will have no meaning.

The consequences of behavior – good or bad – is how dogs learn to associate the command with the desired action. The word "Come" should always mean something pleasurable for your puppy. You should invest a lot of time teaching a recall.

- Practise calling your puppy in the house, and in the garden, encouraging him to come to you. Never grab at him if he runs past you, as it will become a game of 'keep away'.
- Call your puppy to you often, touch his collar, and give him a treat.
- When you take him out, do not fall into the trap of only calling him back to put on his lead and end his games. It will not take long for an intelligent German Shepherd to ignore the recall command because it means the end of fun.
- Instead, during an off-lead walk, regularly call him back, reward him, and then send him off again. Sometimes put the lead on, walk a few paces, remove the lead and play with him.

Unless you are certain your dog will come away from distractions, keep him on a long training line (approx 33 ft/10 m in length) to prevent him disobeying your recall command. You can let him drag the line or you can hold the end. If he ignores your recall command, give a little tug on the line, call him in a happy or upbeat tone, and encourage him to come right up to you. Immediately reward his return.

Do not let bad habits develop by allowing your dog to choose not to come when he is called, or punishing when he does eventually return to you. Practise calling him to you in lots of different places. A good way of building up a strong response to the recall is to ask someone to hold your dog and then call him to you.

If you have a reliable recall your Shepherd will benefit as you will be able to allow him greater freedom.

Stationary exercises

The "Sit" and "Down" commands are not difficult to teach if you are using positive rewards; even a very young puppy is capable of understanding. Work on these before progressing to the "Stay" exercise.

Sit: step by step

- Hold a treat in front of your puppy's nose, and raise the treat up and very slightly back over his head. As he looks up, he will drop into a Sit. As soon as he sits, reward him.
- Repeat several times, and then introduce the word "Sit" as he drops into position.
- Do the same at mealtimes. Hold his bowl up, tell him to "Sit" and feed him. He will soon automatically sit before being fed.

Down: step by step

- Start with your puppy in a Sit. Hold a treat under his nose, place your other hand gently on his shoulders, and slowly lower the treat to the ground between his paws. The treat will lure him into the down position.
- Keep your hand over the treat until your puppy lies down. Reward by letting him eat the treat on the ground between his paws. This will encourage him to keep his head near the floor rather than follow your hand for the reward.
- Introduce the command "Down" as he drops to the floor.

As well as luring your puppy into position, you can teach him to associate the word with the action by simply watching for him to sit or lie down naturally, say "Sit" or "Down" as he goes into position, and then reward him. If you are using a clicker, click at the exact moment he sits or drops into a Down, and then give him a treat.

When your puppy is going into these positions on command, practise getting him to sit or lie down before you give him something he wants – such as a favorite toy, going out of the door, fetching a ball etc. Practise in many different places.

Stay: step by step

Teaching a solid stay takes time and patience. A puppy does not have the necessary self control to stay for very long. A careful introduction to the concept of staying in one place until given a release command will result in a dog that is confident and reliable to the command "Stay". Do not start teaching this exercise when your puppy is excited or wanting to play. Wait until he is calm and relaxed.

- Start by teaching him to stay in the Down position, first making sure there are no distractions or anything in the environment that could frighten him.
- With the puppy in the Down, say "Stay" and wait two seconds. Reward him and say your release word, "OK".
- Repeat a few times, gradually increasing the time before rewarding. Be close to the puppy because, at this stage, you are building up time not distance. You are positively reinforcing the Down-stay by rewarding him in position.

- Sometimes wait four seconds and then say "Stay"; wait another three seconds, reward, then release with "OK".
- When your puppy will stay down for 15-10 seconds, you can begin to add some distance. Tell him "Down-stay", take a step away, wait for five seconds, return, and reward for release.

- Repeat a few times. Then, if all is going well, take three steps away and wait for five seconds. This must be taught slowly. Give him confidence when he is staying, by gently saying "Stay" and "Good boy" to reinforce the position. This will also keep his attention on you.

Stopping unacceptable behavior

There will times when you need to call a halt to unacceptable behaviour. This should not be done in anger or frustration. In order that your dog sees you as a strong pack leader, you must react in a calm but firm manner.

"No" is urgent and should be instantly obeyed. "Leave" is a command taught as a basic 'good manners' behavior.

No: step by step

- "No" is taught as a correction. The unwanted behavior must be interrupted and then the dog's attention should be redirected back to you.

- The type of interruption depends on the situation.
- A quick movement towards the dog as you say "No" in a deep, firm voice may be sufficient to stop him.
- You may need to use a loud sound, such as a can with a few pebbles inside, which will make a sharp noise when shaken.
- Whatever you use as an interrupter to stop the behavior must immediately be followed with praise and reward, communicating to the dog that he is now behaving in an acceptable manner.

The key element of correction is surprise, not pain. It should be split-second and instantly effective; it must be given calmly followed by positive reinforcement when the dog's behavior is correct. An example of an unwanted behavior that can be stopped using an interrupter is mouthing by a puppy or young dog. Correction should never be used when teaching your dog a new behavior.

Control exercises

These are important lessons, teaching your Shepherd to respond to your wishes – even when he has something he does not want to give up.

Leave: step by step

You cannot expect your puppy to leave something when you tell him unless he knows what it means.

- Ask your puppy to "Sit", give him a small treat, and then hold another one between your finger and thumb.
- Tell him to "Leave" in a calm voice and close your hand over the treat, keeping your hand still. If your puppy licks or paws your hand, ignore him.
- Only say "Leave" once. Be patient and wait until he moves his head away from your hand and then immediately give him the treat.

- Repeat this several times. Your puppy will soon work out that he must move his head away when you say "Leave" to get his treat.
- Gradually build the time he has to wait for the treat without mugging you before rewarding him.
- Once you can see he understands the word "Leave", use it with other items. As soon as he responds correctly, reward him.

If you want your puppy to relinquish something in his mouth, teach "Drop" or "Leave" for a treat or a more exciting game with a different toy.

- Hold a treat in front of his nose.

- As soon as he loosens his grip on the toy to get the treat, say "Drop" or "Leave".
- Catch the toy in your hand as you praise him and give him the treat. As soon as he has finished, let him have the toy back to continue the game, as this is also a reward for giving it up on command.
- Practise in quick, short sessions, and he will soon be happy to obey your command.

Wait: step by step

This exercise is all about self-control; it means your dog should wait calmly until you tell him to do something else. He must wait while a door or garden gate is opened, wait to go in or out of the car, and wait before a toy is thrown. "Wait" helps the dog to understand that you are in control of what he wants. I like my dogs to make eye contact with me before being released from the "Wait" command.

- Initially, say "Wait" and make a little sound, something like clicking with your tongue.
- As your puppy looks at you to investigate the sound, immediately give him permission to do what he was waiting to do.
- Repeat this for different situations, gradually extending the waiting time before the release.

"Wait" means stay in position until the next command is given.

The ideal owner

There are many attributes that I could list to describe the ideal owner of a German Shepherd, including everything previously mentioned regarding enhancing your training and handling skills. Here are some essentials:

- An ideal owner is consistent and decisive, patient and emotionally disciplined.
- We must be in control, and the dog must know we have control.
- We must be fair pack leaders, teaching our German Shepherds to live in harmony with us out of respect and trust, never fear.
- We must have a sense of humour and appreciate that a dog is just a dog; he has no sense of fair play, and does nothing out of spite. Our own anger or life's frustrations must never be taken out upon

the dog, as this compromises the quality of our relationship with him.

As a training instructor, I have been saddened to see the utter confusion in a dog due to his owner's impatience, harshness and even punishment because the dog cannot work out what is wanted. An ideal German Shepherd owner will understand that communication is two-way and will endeavour to give the dog clear instructions in a way he can understand.

Opportunities for German Shepherds

There are many activities at which a German Shepherd excels and you can enjoy sharing. The mental and physical stimulation of these activities is a challenge he will thrive on.

Agility

Agility is a fast and fun activity; both the handler and dog have to be fit, and your German Shepherd must be under control. To learn to use the equipment you will need to find a club that specializes in the sport. The set agility course is over a series of obstacles, which includes jumps (upright and long), weaving poles, A-frame, dog walk, seesaw, and tunnels. All of this is done at speed with the winner completing the course in the fastest time with the fewest faults.

The show ring

If your dog is a good example of the breed and conforms closely to the Breed Standard, you may be interested in showing.

Your first step should be to join a specialist breed club with your puppy to learn about correct conformation and movement, and how to train your dog for his presentation to the judge. There are several levels of dog shows from fun companion shows, where many owners start with their pet as an enjoyable hobby, to the most prestigious specialist breed Championship shows where the German Shepherd will need to be of very high merit to be successful.

Good citizen scheme

Joining a dog club and taking part in the Good Citizen scheme is an excellent foundation for training your puppy or older dog. The scheme is run by American Kennel Club (AKC) in the USA and the Kennel Club in the UK, promoting responsible ownership and socially acceptable dogs.

Obedience

Training your dog in formal obedience can range from regularly attending a training club to competing in competitive obedience shows where you progress through the levels from novice to advanced. Exercises include heelwork, recall, stays, retrieve, scent discrimination, send-away, and distance control. Competitive obedience requires accuracy and precision.

Tracking

The versatile German Shepherd is a good choice for this demanding sport where the dog must learn to follow scent trails of varying age, over different types of terrain. In the US, this is a sport in its own right; in the UK it is incorporated into Working Trials where a dog must also compete in two other elements – control and agility.

Schutzhund

This international sport originated in Germany, with the name deriving from the german word for 'protection dog'. It was designed to test the Shepherd's mental stability, endurance, ability to scent, courage and willingness to work.

Health care

We are fortunate that the German Shepherd is a healthy dog, and with good routine care, a well balanced diet, and sufficient exercise, most dogs will experience few health problems.

However, it is your responsibility to put a programme of preventative health care in place – and this should start from the moment your puppy, or older dog, arrives in his new home.

Vaccinations

Dogs are subject to a number of contagious diseases. In the old days, these were killers, and resulted in heartbreak for many owners. Vaccinations have now been developed, and the occurrence of the major infectious diseases is now very rare. However, this will only remain the case if all pet owners follow a strict policy of vaccinating their dogs.

There are vaccinations available for the following diseases:

Adenovirus: This affects the liver; affected dogs have a classic 'blue eye'.

Distemper: A viral disease which causes chest and gastro-intestinal damage. The brain may also be affected, leading to fits and paralysis.

Parvovirus: Causes severe gastro enteritis, and most commonly affects puppies.

Leptospirosis: This bacterial disease is carried by rats and affects many mammals, including humans. It causes liver and kidney damage.

Rabies: A virus that affects the nervous system and is invariably fatal. The first signs are abnormal behavior when the infected dog may bite another animal or a person. Paralysis and death follow. Vaccination is compulsory in most countries. In the UK, dogs travelling overseas must be vaccinated.

Kennel Cough: There are several strains of Kennel Cough, but they all result in a harsh, dry, cough. This disease is rarely fatal; in fact most dogs make a good recovery within a matter of weeks and show few signs of ill health while they are affected. However, kennel cough is highly infectious among dogs that live together so, for this reason, most boarding kennels will insist that your dog is protected by the vaccine, which is given as nose drops.

Lyme Disease: This is a bacterial disease transmitted by ticks (see page 162). The first signs are limping, but the heart, kidneys and nervous system can also be affected. The ticks that transmit the disease occur in specific regions, such as the north-east states of the USA, some of the southern states, California and the upper Mississippi region. Lyme disease is till rare in the UK so vaccinations are not routinely offered.

Vaccination programme

In the USA, the American Animal Hospital Association advises vaccination for core diseases, which they list as: distemper, adenovirus, parvovirus and rabies. The requirement for vaccinating for non-core diseases – leptospriosis, Lyme disease and kennel cough – should be assessed depending on a dog's individual risk and his likely exposure to the disease. In the UK, vaccinations are routinely given for distemper, adenovirus, leptospirosis and parvo virus.

In most cases, a puppy will start his vaccinations at around eight weeks of age, with the second part given in a fortnight's time. However, this does vary depending on the individual policy of veterinary practices, and the incidence of disease in your area.

You should also talk to your vet about whether to give annual booster vaccinations. This depends on an individual dog's levels of immunity, and how long a particular vaccine remains effective.

Parasites

No matter how well you look after your German Shepherd, you will have to accept that parasites – internal and external – are ever present, and you need to take preventative action.

Internal parasites: As the name suggests, these parasites live inside your dog. Most will find a home in the digestive tract, but there is also a parasite that lives in the heart. If infestation is unchecked, a dog's health will be severely jeopardized, but routine preventative treatment is simple and effective.

External parasites: These live on your dog's body – in his skin and fur, and sometimes in his ears.

Roundworm

This is found in the small intestine, and signs of infestation will be a poor coat, a pot belly, diarrhoea and lethargy. Pregnant mothers should be treated, but it is almost inevitable that parasites will be passed on

Puppies and adults should be routinely treated for internal and external parasites.

to the puppies. For this reason, a breeder will start a worming programme, which you will need to continue. Ask your vet for advice on treatment, which will need to continue throughout your dog's life.

Tapeworm

Infection occurs when fleas and lice are ingested; the adult worm takes up residence in the small intestine, releasing mobile segments (which contain eggs) which can be seen in a dog's feces as small rice-like grains. The only other obvious sign of infestation is irritation of the anus. Again, routine preventative treatment is required throughout your Shepherd's life.

Heartworm

This parasite is transmitted by mosquitoes, and so it is more likely to be present in areas with a warm, humid climate. However, it is found in all parts of the USA, although its prevalence does vary. At present, heartworm is rarely seen in the UK.

Heartworms live in the right side of the heart and larvae can grow up to 14 in (35 cm) in length. A dog with heartworm is at severe risk from heart failure, so preventative treatment, as advised by your vet, is essential. Dogs living in the USA should also have regular blood tests to check for the presence of infection.

Lungworm

Lungworm, or *Angiostrongylus vasorum*, is a parasite that lives in the heart and major blood vessels supplying the lungs. It can cause many problems, such as breathing difficulties, excessive bleeding, sickness and diarrhoea, seizures, and can even be fatal.

The parasite is carried by slugs and snails, and the dog becomes infected when ingesting these, often accidentally when rummaging through undergrowth. Lungworm is not common, but it is on the increase and a responsible owner should be aware of it. Fortunately, it is easily preventable and even affected dogs usually make a full recovery if treated early enough. Your vet will be able to advise you on the risks in your area and what form of treatment may be required.

Fleas

A dog may carry dog fleas, cat fleas, and even human fleas. The flea stays on the dog only long enough to feed and breed, but its presence will cause irritation. If your dog has an allergy to fleas – usually a reaction to the flea's saliva – he will scratch until he is raw.

Spot-on treatment, administered on a routine basis, is easy to use and highly effective. You can also treat your dog with a spray or with insecticidal shampoo. Bear in mind that the whole environment your dog lives in will need to be sprayed, and all other pets living in your home will need to be treated.

How to detect fleas

You may suspect your dog has fleas, but how can you be sure? There are two methods to try.

Run a fine comb through your dog's coat, and see if you can detect the presence of fleas on the skin, or clinging to the comb. Alternatively, sit your dog on some white paper and rub his back. This will dislodge feces from the fleas, which will be visible as small brown specks. To double check, shake the specks on to some damp cotton wool (cotton). Flea feces consists of the dried blood taken from the host, so if the specks turn a lighter shade of red, you know your dog has fleas.

Ticks

These blood-suckers are most frequently found in rural areas where sheep or deer are present. The main danger is their ability to pass Lyme disease to both dogs and humans. Lyme disease is prevalent in some areas of the USA (see page 156), although it is still rare in the UK. You should discuss the level of risk and the best form of treatment with your vet.

How to remove a tick

If you spot a tick on your dog, do not try to pluck it off as you risk leaving the hard mouth parts embedded in his skin. The best way to remove a tick is to use a fine pair of tweezers or you can buy a tick remover. Grasp the tick head firmly and then pull the tick straight out from the skin. If you are using a tick remover, check the instructions, as some recommend a circular twist when pulling. When you have removed the tick, clean the area with mild soap and water.

Ear mites

Signs of infestation with ear mites are a brown, waxy discharge, and your dog will continually shake his head and scratch his ear. If you suspect your Shepherd has ear mites, visit your vet will so that medicated ear drops can be prescribed.

Fur mites

These small, white parasites are visible to the naked eye and are often referred to as 'walking dandruff'. They cause a scurfy coat and mild itchiness. However, they are zoonotic – transferable to humans – so prompt treatment with an insecticide prescribed by your vet is essential.

Harvest mites

These are picked up from the undergrowth, and can be seen as a bright orange patch on the webbing between the toes, although this can also be found elsewhere on the body, such as on the ears flaps. Treatment is effective with the appropriate insecticide.

Skin mites

There are two types of parasite that burrow into a dog's skin. Demodex canis is transferred from a mother to her pups while they are feeding. Treatment is with a topical preparation, and sometimes antibiotics are needed.

The other skin mite, sarcoptes scabiei, causes intense itching and hair loss. It is highly contagious, so all dogs in a household will need to be treated, which involves repeated bathing with a medicated shampoo.

Common ailments

As with all living animals, dogs can be affected by a variety of ailments, most of which can be treated effectively by your vet, who will advise you on how to care for your dog's needs.

Anal glands

These are two small sacs on either side of the anus, which produce a dark-brown secretion that dogs use when they mark their territory. The anal glands should empty every time a dog defecates but, if they become blocked or impacted, a dog will experience increasing discomfort. He may nibble at his rear end, or 'scoot' his bottom along the ground to relieve the irritation.

Treatment involves a trip to the vet where the vet will empty the glands manually. It is important to do this without delay or infection may occur.

See Anal Furunculosis, page 177.

Dental problems

Good dental hygiene will do much to minimize problems with gum infection and tooth decay. If tartar accumulates to the extent that you cannot remove it by brushing, the vet will need to intervene. In a situation such as this, an anesthetic will need to be administered so the tartar can be removed manually.

Diarrhoea

There are many reasons why a dog has diarrhoea, but most commonly it is the result of scavenging, a sudden change of diet, or an adverse reaction to a particular type of food.

If your dog is suffering from diarrhoea, the first step is to withdraw food for a day. It is important that he does not dehydrate, so make sure that fresh drinking water is available. However, drinking too much can increase the diarrhoea, which may be accompanied with vomiting, so limit how much he drinks at any one time.

After allowing the stomach to rest, feed a bland diet, such as white fish or chicken with boiled rice for a few days. In most cases, your dog's motions will return to normal and you can resume normal feeding, although this should be done gradually.

See Exocrine Pancreatic Insufficiency, page 181.

Ear infections

The German Shepherd has erect ears, which allow the air to circulate, thus reducing the risk of ear infections.

A healthy ear is clean with no sign of redness or inflammation, and no evidence of a waxy brown discharge or a foul odor. If you see your dog scratching his ear, shaking his head, or holding one ear at an odd angle, you will need to consult your vet.

The most likely causes are ear mites (see page 163), an infection, or there may a foreign body, such as a grass seed, trapped in the ear.

Depending on the cause, treatment is with medicated ear drops, possibly containing antibiotics. If a foreign body is suspected, the vet will need to carry our further investigations.

Eye problems

If your Shepherd's eyes look red and sore, he may be suffering from Conjunctivitis. This may, or may not be accompanied with a watery or a crusty discharge.

Conjunctivitis can be caused by a bacterial or viral infection, it could be the result of an injury, or it could be an adverse reaction to pollen.

You will need to consult your vet for a correct diagnosis, but in the case of an infection, treatment with medicated eye drops is effective.

Conjunctivitis may also be the first sign of more serious inherited eye problems, see page 182.

Foreign bodies

In the home, puppies – and some older dogs – cannot resist chewing anything that looks interesting. The toys you choose for your dog should be suitably robust to withstand damage, but children's toys can be irresistible. Some dogs will chew – and swallow – anything from socks, tights, and other items from the laundry basket, to golf balls and stones from the garden. Obviously, these items are indigestible and could cause an obstruction in your dog's intestine, which is potentially lethal.

The signs to look for are vomiting, and a tucked up posture. The dog will often be restless and will look as though he is in pain. In this situation, you must get your dog to the vet without delay as surgery will be needed to remove the obstruction.

The other type of foreign body that may cause problems is grass seed. A grass seed can enter an orifice such as a nostril, down an ear, the gap between the eye and the eyelid, or penetrate the soft skin between the toes. It can also be swallowed.

The introduction of a foreign body induces a variety of symptoms, depending on the point of entry and where it travels to. The signs to look for include head shaking/ear scratching, the eruption of an abscess, sore, inflamed eyes, or a persistent cough. The vet will be able to make a proper diagnosis, and surgery may be required.

Heat stroke

This is a condition that can affect a dog literally within minutes; the greatest danger is if a dog is confined in a car with insufficient ventilation. The temperature can rise dramatically – even on a cloudy day – and unless you are able lower your dog's temperature, it can be fatal.

If your Shepherd appears to be suffering from heatstroke, lie him flat., and then cool him as quickly as possible by hosing him, covering him with wet towels, or using frozen food bags from the freezer. As soon as he has made some recovery, take him to the vet where cold intravenous fluids can be administered.

Lameness/ limping

There are a wide variety of reasons why a dog can go lame, from a simple muscle strain to a fracture, ligament damage, or more complex problems with the joints. It takes an expert to make a correct diagnosis, so if you are concerned about your dog, do not delay in seeking help.

The German Shepherd is prone to a number of breed specific conditions which result in lameness, so extra vigilance is required, and care should be taken not to over-exercise a growing dog.

For more information on these conditions, see Degenerative Myelopathy (page 178), Elbow Dysplasia (page 178), Hip Dysplasia (page 184), and Panosteitis (page 186).

As your Shepherd becomes elderly, he may suffer from arthritis, which you will see as general stiffness, particularly when he gets up after resting. It will help if you ensure his bed is in a warm, draught-free location, and, if your Shepherd gets wet after exercise, you must dry him thoroughly.

If your Shepherd seems to be in pain, consult your vet who will be able to help with pain relief medication.

Skin problems

If your dog is scratching or nibbling at his skin, the first thing to check for is fleas (see page 163). There are other parasites which cause itching and hair loss, but you will need a vet to help you find the culprit.

An allergic reaction is another major cause of skin problems. It can be quite an undertaking to find the cause of the allergy, and you will need to follow your vet's advice.

Inherited & breed-disposed disorders

The German Shepherd does have some breed-related disorders. If diagnosed with any of the diseases listed below, it is important to remember that they can affect offspring, so breeding from affected dogs should be discouraged.

There are now recognized screening tests to enable breeders to check for affected individuals and hence reduce the prevalence of these diseases within the breed.

For details of the organizations concerned, see page 180 and 182.

DNA testing is also becoming more widely available, and as research into the different genetic diseases progresses, more DNA tests are being developed.

All breeding stock should be subjected to health clearances.

Anal furunculosis

This is a very painful disease of the tissues around the anus. There could be a genetic factor. The first sign is the dog constantly licking around the anal area, and, on inspection, small oozing sores can be seen around the anus. These will have already become deep, painful fistulas and it may be difficult to examine the dog due to the pain.

Veterinary treatment includes antibiotic therapy and surgical removal of all the infected tissue. If this condition is caught early, treatment may be more successful. It seems to develop in middle-aged dogs. German Shepherd owners need to check under the dog's tail regularly to make sure the anal area is clear.

Degenerative myelopathy (DM)

DM is a degenerative neurological disease seen primarily in the German Shepherd over 5 years old. Clinical signs can begin as dragging toes and scuffing nails and progress to caudal spinal and hind limb weakness, which may either wane or steadily worsen.

There is no curative treatment, but dietary supplements, controlled exercise and supportive carts have all been used to help enable a good quality of life. There is a DNA test available to prevent future generations being affected.

Elbow dysplasia

This is a developmental disease where the elbow does not mature correctly and signs of lameness are usually seen in younger, large breed dogs. It can affect one or both elbows, and covers several different types of condition, which can present as one or more of the following, at the same time:

Ununited anconeal process usually develops between the ages of five to seven months when a fragment of bone of the joint does not unite with the ulna

during growth. It is first noticed as foreleg lameness. Fragmented medial coronoid process (FMCP) is when a small piece of bone lies loose in the joint, causing pain and lameness.

Osteochondritis dissecans (OCD) and osteochondrosis (OC) are caused when a piece of cartilage becomes partially or fully detached from the growing bone. Usually the elbow or shoulder joint is affected, but the hock joint on the back leg can also develop the problem.

In the US, X-rays are submitted to the Orthopedic Foundation for Animals; in the UK X-rays are sent to the British Veterinary Association where a panel will give a grading to each elbow. Severely affected dogs should not be used for breeding.

Surgery may be indicated to correct the abnormalities, but the affected joints will be more prone to arthritis later in life.

Epilepsy

This is an inherited condition in the Shepherd, often first seen as seizures occurring in the younger or middle-aged dog. Treatment is usually in the form of lifelong anticonvulsant medication to control the seizures. Each dog needs to be individually monitored to ensure the right level of medication is being used.

Exocrine pancreatic insufficiency

This is a common condition, which has a hereditary basis, and has a higher prevalence in the German Shepherd. EPI is an inadequate production of digestive enzymes, resulting in malabsorption, especially of fats, and chronic diarrhoea, which is grey-colored and foul-smelling. Despite a ravenous appetite, weight loss will be extreme. A simple blood test (TLI) will confirm the diagnosis.

Dogs can show a good response to treatment and live a fairly normal life, but affected dogs should not be used for breeding.

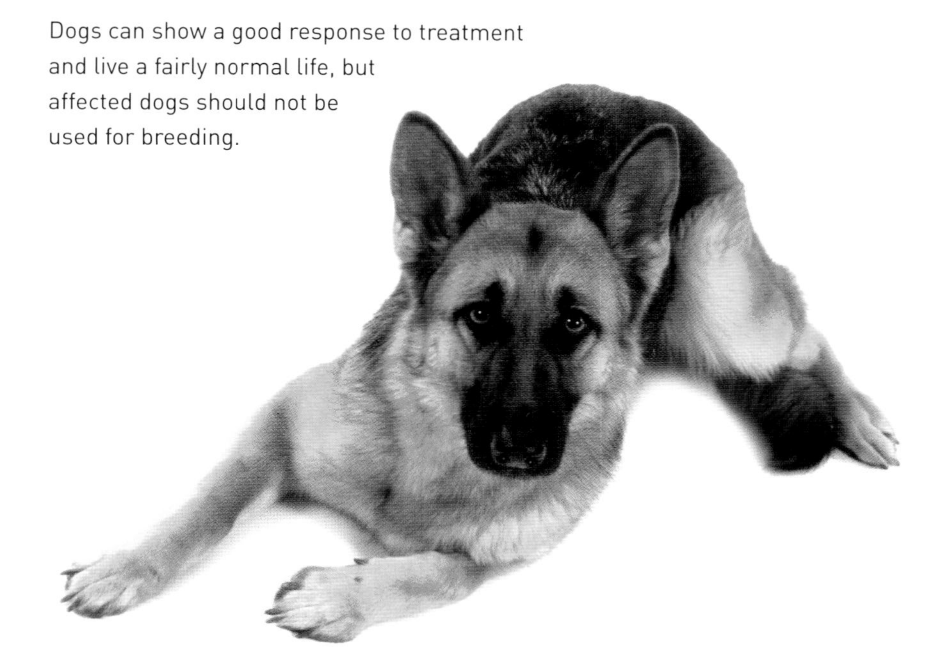

Eye disorders

Multifocal retinal dysplasia: This is the abnormal development of the retina. The mildest form has minimal effect on vision, but severe forms may manifest as complete retinal detachment and blindness. Retinal dysplasia is identified by an eye examination by the Canine Eye Registration Foundation in the US, and as part of the British Veterinary Association/Kennel Club, International Sheep Dog Society eye scheme in the UK.

Hereditary cataracts: German Shepherds can suffer from hereditary cataracts where the lens is often affected in younger dogs but may not be evident until later in life. There are varying degrees of severity. The inherited form usually has little effect on eyesight but, if necessary, surgery is usually successful. Screening is available with the organizations mentioned above.

Gastric dilation/volvulus

This condition, commonly known as bloat or gastric torsion, is where the stomach swells visibly (dilatation) and then rotates (volvulus), so that the exit into the small intestine becomes blocked, preventing food from leaving. This results in stomach pain and a bloated abdomen. It is a severe, life-threatening condition that requires immediate

veterinary attention (usually surgery) to decompress and return the stomach to its normal position.

There appears to be several risk factors causing the development of GDV and by taking the following precautions, you can reduce the risk.

* Feed two smaller meals per day instead one large one.
* Do not allow the dog to drink a large volume of water at one time.
* Do not feed immediately before or after strenuous exercise – wait at least two hours.

Hemophilia A

This is a blood-clotting defect that affects males; females can be carriers but are not affected. It is an inherited disorder where there is a deficiency in Factor VIII, one of the factors involved in the clotting cascade. This results in bleeding with any traumatic incident which, if severe, can be life-threatening. There are blood tests available to detect carriers to help prevent the disease affecting future generations.

Hip dysplasia

Perhaps the most well-known health issue in the breed is hip dysplasia. This is any abnormality of one or both hip joints. In severe cases, the dog shows considerable pain, stiffness when getting up, lameness and has difficulty walking. Mildly affected dogs may show no signs and lead a normal life, but arthritis of the joints may develop in later life.

Although known to be hereditary, environmental effects during the rapid growth phase of a young dog, such as over-exercise, excessive weight and poor nutrition, can contribute. Gentle exercise, reduction in obesity, anti-inflammatory drugs and home management are all part of the treatment regimes used to control the disease.

In the US, hip scoring is carried out by the Orthopedic Foundation for Animals. X-rays are submitted when a dog is two years old, categorized as Normal (Excellent, Good, Fair), Borderline, and Dysplastic (Mild, Moderate, Severe). The hip grades of Excellent, Good and Fair are within normal limits and are given OFA numbers.

In the UK, the minimum age for the hips to be assessed by X-ray is 12 months. Each hip can score between 0 (best) to 53 (worst). Both left and right scores are added together to give the total hip score.

Juvenile renal dysplasia

This is a hereditary disease found in the German Shepherd, causing incorrect development of the kidneys, and, in severe cases, renal failure in young dogs. If only mildly affected, there may be no clinical signs obvious and these carriers have the potential to pass on the defect to future generations. There is no treatment, but a DNA test is available to identify affected individuals and prevent the disease from occurring in future generations.

Panosteitis

This is a cause of sudden, severe lameness, which can alternate from one leg to another. The cause of this is unknown, but dogs often have a high temperature at the same time and a virus is suspected. The disease will usually resolve with time, but if signs are severe, then rest and anti-inflammatories can be used.

Pituitary dwarfism

In this condition, the German Shepherd puppy suffers from a failure to produce enough growth hormone, which will result in stunted growth, although the dog does stay in proportion. This inherited condition also results in a woolly, puppy-like coat, which is easily lost, and dark skin on the

hairless areas. Often, affected individuals suffer from a shortened life span despite medication.

A DNA test is available to determine genetically affected individual carriers to enable breeders to avoid reproducing this disease in future generations.

Von Willebrand's Disease

This disease is characterized by a deficiency in von Willebrand's factor (vWF), which is vital to help platelets form clots and stop bleeding.

There are three types – I, II and III – with a corresponding increase in severity with increasing number. German Shepherds are most commonly affected by type I, where there is less than 50% of the normal amount of vWF.

This condition is quite widespread in the USA and is also associated with the Doberman.

Summing Up

Although it may raise concerns to find out about health problems that may affect your German Shepherd, it is important to bear in mind that acquiring some basic knowledge is an invaluable asset, as it will allow you to spot signs of trouble at an early stage. Early diagnosis is very often the means to the most effective treatment.

It would be wise, when choosing your German Shepherd, to be aware of the potential problems and to ensure that the parent dogs have already been tested for the most severe and prevalent diseases, thereby reducing the likelihood in your GSD.

Useful addresses

Breed Kennel Clubs
Please contact your Kennel Club to obtain contact information about breed clubs in your area.

UK
The Kennel Club (UK)
1 Clarges Street London, W1J 8AB
Telephone: 0870 606 6750
Fax: 0207 518 1058
Web: www.thekennelclub.org.uk

USA
American Kennel Club (AKC)
5580 Centerview Drive, Raleigh, NC 27606.
Telephone: 919 233 9767
Fax: 919 233 3627
Email: info@akc.org
Web: www.akc.org

United Kennel Club (UKC)
100 E Kilgore Rd, Kalamazoo,
MI 49002-5584, USA.
Tel: 269 343 9020
Fax: 269 343 7037
Web:www.ukcdogs.com

Australia
Australian National Kennel Council (ANKC)
The Australian National Kennel Council is the administrative body for pure breed canine affairs in Australia. It does not, however, deal directly with dog exhibitors, breeders or judges. For information pertaining to breeders, clubs or shows, please contact the relevant State or Territory Body.

International
Fédération Cynologique Internationalé (FCI)
Place Albert 1er, 13, B-6530 Thuin, Belgium.
Tel: +32 71 59.12.38
Fax: +32 71 59.22.29
Web: www.fci.be

Training and behavior
UK
Association of Pet Dog Trainers
Telephone: 01285 810811
Web: www.apdt.co.uk

Association of Pet Behaviour Counsellors
Telephone: 01386 751151
Web: www.apbc.org.uk

USA
Association of Pet Dog Trainers
Tel: 1 800 738 3647
Web: www.apdt.com

American College of Veterinary Behaviorists
Web: www.dacvb.org

American Veterinary Society of Animal Behavior
Web: www.avsabonline.org

Australia
APDT Australia Inc
Web: www.apdt.com.au

Canine Behavior
For details of regional behvaiorists, contact the relevant State or Territory Controlling Body.

Activities

UK

Agility Club
Web: www.agilityclub.co.uk

British Flyball Association
Telephone: 01628 829623
Web: www.flyball.org.uk

USA

North American Dog Agility Council
Web: www.nadac.com

North American Flyball Association, Inc.
Tel/Fax: 800 318 6312
Web: www.flyball.org

Australia

Agility Dog Association of Australia
Tel: 0423 138 914
Web: www.adaa.com.au

NADAC Australia
Web: www.nadacaustralia.com

Australian Flyball Association
Tel: 0407 337 939
Web: www.flyball.org.au

International

World Canine Freestyle Organisation
Tel: (718) 332-8336
Web: www.worldcaninefreestyle.org

Health

UK

British Small Animal Veterinary Association
Tel: 01452 726700
Web: www.bsava.com

Royal College of Veterinary Surgeons
Tel: 0207 222 2001
Web: www.rcvs.org.uk

www.dogbooksonline.co.uk/healthcare

Alternative Veterinary Medicine Centre
Tel: 01367 710324
Web: www.alternativevet.or

USA

American Veterinary Medical Association
Tel: 800 248 2862
Web: www.avma.org

American College of Veterinary Surgeons
Tel: 301 916 0200
Toll Free: 877 217 2287
Web: www.acvs.org

Canine Eye Registration Foundation
The Veterinary Medical DataBases
1717 Philo Rd, PO Box 3007,
Urbana, IL 61803-3007
Tel: 217-693-4800
Fax: 217-693-4801
Web: www.vmdb.org/cerf.html

Orthopaedic Foundation of Animals
2300 E Nifong Boulevard
Columbia, Missouri, 65201-3806
Tel: 573 442-0418
Fax: 573 875-5073
Web: www.offa.org

American Holistic Veterinary Medical Association
Tel: 410 569 0795
Web: www.ahvma.org

Australia

Australian Small Animal Veterinary Association
Tel: 02 9431 5090
Web: www.asava.com.au

Australian Veterinary Association
Tel: 02 9431 5000
Web: www.ava.com.au

Australian College Veterinary Scientists
Tel: 07 3423 2016
Web: www.acvsc.org.au

Australian Holistic Vets
Web: www.ahv.com.au